IN MEMORIAM:

A MEMORIAL OF

VERSAL JESSE WALKER, M. A.

PROFESSOR OF THE LATIN LANGUAGE AND LITERATURE

IN THE

UNIVERSITY OF MINNESOTA.

Suis dilectis sic dat somnum.

PUBLISHED BY THE UNIVERSITY

1876.

RESOLUTIONS OF THE FACULTY.

UNIVERSITY OF MINNESOTA,
Minneapolis, May 24, 1876.

TO THE GENERAL FACULTY OF THE UNIVERSITY :—Your committee, to whom was referred the preparation of resolutions commemorative of Professor V. J. Walker, beg leave to submit the following:

WHEREAS, Our Heavenly Father in the mysterious wisdom of His Providence has removed from us by the hand of death our fellow laborer, Professor Versal J. Walker; and,

WHEREAS, We recognize in this sad event the loss to the University of Minnesota of a wise counsellor and an instructor of unusual faithfulness and ability, and to us, his associates, of a congenial brother and an upright Christian man ; therefore,

Resolved, That we tender our heartfelt sympathies to the bereaved relatives of the deceased, especially to the sorrowing wife and mother ; and that we prepare and publish a memorial pamphlet which shall becomingly commemorate the worth of our lamented friend.

Resolved, That a copy of these resolutions be presented to the family of the deceased, and that they be published in the Pioneer-Press and Tribune, Minneapolis Tribune, and Winona Republican.

G. CAMPBELL,
JABEZ BROOKS,
E. J. THOMPSON,
Committee.

NOTE.—These resolutions were unanimously adopted and entered on the records. The Faculty also designated the above committee to prepare and publish an appropriate memorial pamphlet, in accordance with the foregoing resolution.

In Memoriam.

BIOGRAPHICAL SKETCH.

Professor Versal J. Walker was born in Brookline, in the State of Vermont, in the year 1824, and received an academic education at the Townsend Academy in the same State.

He entered Waterville College (now Colby University) in the State of Maine in the year 1845, from which he graduated in 1849 with the honors of his class. While in college he was particularly distinguished for his proficiency in the sciences and mathematics, although at the same time he took high rank in the languages.

Soon after graduating he was chosen Principal of the Academy at New-London, New Hampshire. A few years later he took charge of the academy at China in the State of Maine. He continued in the work of teaching at several places in New England until 1855, when he went to California where he remained four years engaged in teaching and in business. He was chosen to an important position in one of the leading institutions of learning in San Francisco; but at the time he was unable to accept it.

Upon his return from California in 1859 he was married to Miss Susan P. Hanscombe, who now survives him. During this year he came to Minnesota and located in Winona, where he immediately entered upon the profession of teaching.

The present excellent school system at Winona, which is excelled by none in the State, and by few in the country, is due largely to Professor Walker's superior ability as an organizer and instructor. He established the first High School in that city and was its Principal for a number of years. He was afterward elected to the joint office of Principal of the High School and Superintendent of the city schools in the same city, which position he filled with great acceptance, until he was elected to the Professorship of the Latin language in the University of Minnesota in 1869. This position he accepted; he honored it with marked ability and acknowledged success until his death.

For several years Professor Walker was Secretary of the State Educational Association and at one time its President. He was one of the few who never sought office, but who always gave character to positions of trust and responsibility. For three years he was a member of the Board of Education of Minneapolis, East Division, during which time he filled the office of Secretary of the Board and discharged the duties of Superintendent of the schools. Under his management the schools were decidedly improved and very prosperous. The governing principle of his life was to do well and thoroughly everything he undertook. The secret of his successful life is found in this one fact—that he was always ready to meet the demand of each hour, each day. Every period of his life might be called a finished life. He brought few if any burdens from the past to oppress, distract and weaken him in the present. And when on May 17, 1876, the summons came bidding him go up higher—he was ready—the day's work was done—his life-work was completed, thoroughly, faithfully and well. Nothing remained but to enter into his reward. He approached the grave

> "sustained and soothed
> By an unfaltering trust"——
> "Like one who wraps the drapery of his couch
> About him, and lies down to pleasant dreams."

FUNERAL SERVICES.

On the morning of Thursday, the 17th of May, President Folwell called a special meeting of the General Faculty of the University and announced to the members present the sad intelligence of the death of Versal J. Walker, Professor of the Latin Language and Literature, which had occurred but a few hours previously. It was unanimously resolved to suspend the usual exercises of the University until after the funeral which was to take place on the following Saturday. The Faculty appointed a committee consisting of Professors Campbell, Brooks, and Thompson to make the proper arrangements for the funeral services. It was decided that members of the faculty should act as pall bearers, and Professors Winchell, Rhame, Peckham, Marston, Moore, and Laing were designated to perform this duty. On Saturday morning the Regents, Faculty and students assembled in the chapel of the University, which was draped in mourning, as was also Professor Walker's class room and desk, and, after the usual religious exercises, marched in a body to the residence of the deceased; Mr. John S. Clarke of the senior class acting as marshal, faculty and students wearing a badge of mourning upon the left arm. At the house the university choir sang "Nearer my God to Thee," and prayer was offered by the Rev. A. A. Russell of the Baptist church. The family, friends and students then took a farewell look at their valued friend and faithful teacher. The procession reformed thereupon in order to proceed to the First Congregational church. The Regents and Faculty in carriages, kindly furnished by his Excellency, Gov. J. S. Pillsbury, were followed by the students in the order of their classes.

At the church the services consisted of singing by the university choir, reading of the Scriptures by Rev. E. M. Williams, prayer by Rev. D. Burt, State Superintendent of Public Instruction, followed by short addresses by Rev. Mr. Russell, Superintendent Burt, Professors Thompson, Brooks and Campbell, and President Folwell.

After the close of the services at the church, the procession, accompanied by a large number of citizens, followed the remains to the cemetery where the choir sang the hymn "He sweetly sleeps," and the benediction was pronounced. The floral testimonials both at the house and the church, were profuse and beautiful. At the church the senior class had provided a broken column from the top of which was growing the fadeless ivy. The junior class furnished an anchor of flowers, the sophomores a cross and crown; while the freshmen and other classes brought bouquets, baskets and wreaths in rich abundance. The general arrangements were directed by Dr. J. F. Townsend, the floral decorations being under the charge of Professor P. M. Woodman, assisted by Mrs. Townsend and Mrs. Pillsbury. The grave was lined with evergreens, carpeted and bordered with flowers, by the teachers of the public schools; so that, when we laid him down, he slept amid the flowers—his bed was "soft as downy pillows are."

The following are the names of the University choir who provided the music on the occasion of the funeral of Professor Walker: Tenor, Messrs. E. R. Pritchard and T. B. Columbia; alto, Misses E. B. Whitney and C. L. Chamberlain; soprano, Misses Mattie A. Butler and Mary Robinson; bass, Messrs. J. N. Childs and E. A. Currie; organist, Miss Ida Neher.

REMARKS OF REV. A. A. RUSSELL.

One has represented an angel in tears. Surprise is expressed that an angel should be weeping, and the explanation is, "It is the angel of the earth; he is always weeping." Surely if this angel ever sheds tears of special bitterness he must be doing so on this occasion.

What man could have been taken away who would have been so universally missed in this community as Professor Walker? Would that this event were only a dream! Alas, it is a sad reality! Professor Walker is not asleep on his couch to waken ere long and give us the wonted genuine greeting of genial friendship. He is in his casket, and great waves of actual affliction are dashing over this assembly. Far out where the waters are deepest and coldest are the relatives of the deceased, and around them the Faculty of which he was a member, the Board of Regents, the students, the church to which he belonged, the teachers of our schools, and the citizens generally. As this storm bursts upon us from a sky which had worn no special foretokens, and the billows roll over us, the important practical question is, *What shall we do?*

Shall we go to *Nature?* Nature is now beautiful in the green and flowery garb of May; and the mottoes which hang in her inviting bowers speak of the power, wisdom and goodness of God. She might for the moment divert the heart from its bereavement, but she has no sources of solid consolation for such sorrow as is here prevailing, and much less a balm to *heal* the wounded heart. Shall we rush out into the *world?* The world never wishes to see us, mid its gayety and excitement, with tearful eyes and bleeding hearts; and instinctively we repel the thought of going there for soul solace.

Shall we go to *philosophy?* Welcome as its services may be

many times, there is no satisfaction in contemplating God or man from a merely philosophic point of view in an hour like this. Even the great men who founded its varied schools found their systems too cold and lifeless to warm and vitalize their souls when death broke into the cherished circles of friendship and love.

Out in this wild storm of sorrow, what *shall* we do! Evidently the only thing we can do, or need to, is to send heavenward the cry of David, "*Lead me to the rock that is higher than I.*" The bible discloses God unto us as a loving *Father*, and tenderly invites us to Him. Listen: "Like as a father pitieth his children, so the Lord pitieth them that fear Him." "Cast thy burden upon the Lord, and He shall sustain thee." Isaiah, speaking of the Lord Jesus Christ, says: "He hath sent me to bind up the broken-hearted —to comfort all that mourn; to appoint unto them that mourn in Zion, to give unto them beauty for ashes, the oil of joy for mourning." When Jesus was on earth He spake for himself in these golden words. "Come unto me all ye that labor and are heavy laden, and I will give you rest." Jesus is the embodiment and manifestation of the heart-nature of our Father in heaven. The loving divinity has taken the loved humanity up to the throne; and the nearness of our nature to the Father in the person of the Son, shows that now the Father can and should be approached, especially, when we would "sorrow as those who have no hope" without his aid. With the heart-nature of God presented to us in the "great High Priest of our profession" let us draw near "with a true heart, in full assurance of faith." Let this loving wife and aged mother, so unutterably afflicted by this event, and the other kindred, and the Faculty and Regents, and students of the university, the church, these teachers, and all of us, go at once to God our Father to be sustained, and to find that,—"Earth hath no sorrow that Heaven cannot heal."

REMARKS OF REGENT BURT, SUPERINTENDENT OF PUBLIC INSTRUCTION.

On an occasion like this it becomes a question, how we should understand the maxim, "*De mortuis nil nisi bonum.*" Professor Walker never sought adulation. He was too modest to praise himself. Indiscriminate laudation and lofty eulogy over his lifeless body, were it animated by its former consciousness, would cause its pale, cold brow to blush in silent protest. We must not attach to this maxim a meaning that the deceased would not have sanctioned.

Yet there is a sense in which it is proper that, "concerning the dead, only what is favorable should be spoken." It is difficult to find perfection in any thing finite. A tree may impress us as beautiful; but if we criticise it with the ideal curve of beauty in mind, we discover imperfections in form and distribution of foliage. It is better for our general gratification not to notice such minor defects. So in reviewing the characters of men of recognized excellencies, our rule of judgment should not be an ideal perfection never found in human beings. In speaking of such men after death, it is proper to call attention to the admirable qualities especially illustrated in their lives.

Mr. Walker came to Minnesota about eighteen years ago. He was employed with his estimable wife, to teach in the public schools of Winona. It was in this capacity that I made his acquaintance; and of certain qualities manifested in that early work, I may briefly speak. As a teacher Mr. Walker possessed an unusual ability for organization.

The earlier schools of Winona had of necessity been very much mixed, and there was an ample field in which to illustrate this special ability. It required astute penetration into the peculiarities and attainments of pupils to assort such mixed material, and determine the place for each. We were, however, soon convinced that Mr. Walker had conceptions of a graded system of schools toward which we might all safely and hopefully aim. After a few years he became superintendent of the growing system whose germ he had helped to plant. To his unassuming work in that early time, the schools of that city are today largely indebted for the rich fruits maturing under the care of other skillful teachers.

There was another noticeable excellence in Mr. Walker as a teacher.

He distinguished the essential from the non-essential, and saw important points in their true relations. Discarding mere verbiage, he aimed to bring his classes to a thorough knowledge of what they studied. "If you know it, you can tell it," was often his remark to a hesitating pupil, verified, if necessary by a lucid explanation forcibly illustrating his maxim. This quality made him master of the idioms of the Latin language, an accurate and elegant translator.

But Mr. Walker's success in school management resulted from higher qualities.

He governed by the force of moral ideas. Several of his pupils once devised a plot by which they made the school-room a scene of confusion for several minutes after recess should have terminated. Waiting with calm dignity until the artificially induced sneezing ceased, he remarked for substance in that incisive style of which he was capable, The school has lost ten minutes by the misconduct of two boys. They have tried to diminish their guilt by involving others in their mischief; but I shall hold each one responsible for the entire result—and before the matter ended, the boys found what that meant. The import of this theory of personal ill desert, which I heard him re-state a few days before his death, will appea in his own words. "It is impossible to escape or diminish guilt by splitting a sin into parts, and attempting to divide the responsibility among a large number." It was this view of personal responsibility that gave the deceased much of his moral power as a disciplinarian. Yet there was no terror in his rule. "We were afraid of Mr. Walker but we all loved him." "He was always kind, no matter how severe he was obliged to be," are expressions by those who have been under his gentle, firm moral control.

But such a character is not the result of fortuitous forces. Mr. Walker possessed an inner, spiritual life, and he wrought through its power.

In those early years at Winona, he was at one time prostrated by incipient action of the disease that has finally cut him off from the living. Calling at his room, I learned that he doubted whether he could recover. It was his wish that there might be prayer for his restoration. Gradually he did recover. After entering upon his work again, he seemed to me to regard his life as the prophet Jeremiah must have regarded the fifteen years added to his days in answer to prayer. His subsequent labors have evinced an earnestness of purpose, a serene and constant faith, growing brighter and stronger as he passed away.

Having been requested to represent the Board of Regents on this occasion, I must say that we are deeply afflicted by the sudden death of Professor Walker. His success has been so marked that it will be difficult to fill his place; not because there are no men equal to him in scholarship, but because we may not find in men available for his chair the combination of learning and sound judgment and practical wisdom that marked his course. But the Regents are more than mourners in their official capacity. The departed not only deserved their confidence, but he received their love. They feel his loss socially and realize how severely it falls upon his devoted wife and aged mother, and in behalf of the Regents, I tender to them all the consolation that human sympathy can offer.

In conclusion, I must express the conviction that those who die in the ranks of our Faculty, should not be interred so far from the University that their graves will seldom be visited by students. The graves of Moses Stuart and of Bela B. Edwards, within sight of the Seminary at Andover, preserve and declare its early history, inciting students who never saw those men, to high and noble endeavor.

The University of Minnesota should not detract from the posthumous influence of its faithful dead by interring their remains at a distance from its grounds. Other members of the Faculty may soon follow their departed brother. As time rolls away similar deaths must occur, for "we all do fade as a leaf." We should therefore, select a suitable repository for the ashes of those who may die in the service of the University. It should be a place easy and convenient of access, where, at the sunset hour and in the still twilight, students can saunter and make pilgrimages into the solemn, past and be inspired by its hallowed influences for the great mission of life. How worthy of such sepulture are the sacred contents of the casket before us; and how inspiring the Divine utterance, "The righteous shall be had in everlasting rememberance." This sublime declaration will be made to the students of to-day, and it shall be made to the students of the coming future at the grave of Professor Walker.

REMARKS OF PROFESSOR THOMPSON.

I have been told that the severest moment in the strife of battle was when a brother soldier who was standing shoulder to shoulder in the conflict fell dead at your side. Today I realize that this is truly so. As I look upon the loved and honored form of him who has fallen at my side I feel indeed that he was a brother soldier in more than one respect. He was a brother who years ago took me, a stranger, by the hand and welcomed me to the ranks of the teachers in Minnesota; and in later years, he has been a brother in the ranks of the Professors of the University. He was also a brother in the grand and glorious fraternity of Masons which he very much honored and respected. But better than all, he was a brother in that grander and more glorious Fraternity—the Christian brotherhood which he deeply loved and the prosperity of which he dearly prized.

Upon such an occasion as this, we are apt to study merely the sad event and dwell too much, if possible, on the brevity of life together with the certainty and suddenness of death. But the lesson I would learn at this hour is not only one of sudden death and disappointed hopes, but a lesson from the life of him who has so unexpectedly been taken from us. It is a short but all important lesson; not one of fame, fortune or earthly honors, but a lesson of resolute purpose, faithful trust, and decided success. This lesson I believe is written in imperishable lines on the hearts of hundreds of students who are now before us, as well as upon the hearts of hundreds of others who in different places were Professor Walker's pupils. It is also a lesson of kindness, faithfulness and justice. He was ever kind, faithful and just. He needs no other epitaph. Let only those who have been co-partners with him in the struggle and strife of life attempt to estimate his worth. Such only know its value.

It seems but yesterday since last we met him and asked in brotherly trust his priceless counsel. The day was drawing to a close when worn and weary with the toil and care of anxious work he went to his quiet home, there to receive the affectionate and tender support of a devoted wife and aged mother. This was his last day's work. The summons came bidding him homeward and heavenward. Quickly he obeyed; and now he stands upon the battlements on high, above the toiling and the tiring, the sickening and the dying of mortal life. Well done. Crown the faithful teacher and friend.

REMARKS OF PROFESSOR BROOKS.

There is another moment of painful interest connected with the strifes of battle, besides the one mentioned by Professor Thompson, and which to me seems more sad and bitter; and that is, when the battle is over, and the carnage has ceased, and the decemated ranks stand forth to answer the company or regimental rollcall; then is seen the havoc of death; the unanswered names of fallen comrades fall painfully on the ear. That is a bitter moment. And so, when the Faculty of our University shall assemble again, and the roll be called, one name will receive no response, and we shall bitterly feel the loss of our fallen comrade. "Absent from the body," will be the entry on earthly record, "present with the Lord," will be the new record in heaven.

I would not deal in mere eulogy as I may speak somewhat of the worth of our deceased friend and fellow-laborer; to tell what we know to be true of him is eulogy enough; and none, or few, knew him better than we. My acquaintance with Professor Walker began in 1861, when he was the Principal of the Public Schools in Winona; and we have been associated more or less intimately in educational labors in the State from that time until now. His special labors in Winona have already been sketched. His more general labors—as a member of the State Teachers' Association, of which he was once the President—as a worker in Teachers' Institutes—and as a lecturer on educational subjects—were equally useful and successful. He has helped to give to some of the more important features of our public school system their present efficiency and power. In all these more public relations he endeared himself to his associates by his modesty, his faithfulness, and his unquestioned fitness for his work.

All that the previous speakers have said of the character of Professor Walker is true. He was kind, firm, faithful, true, fearless, outspoken, honest, and just. But the traits of character which impressed me most were his simplicity, and his conscientiousness. His simplicity was very marked. He was simple in his tastes, his dress, his habits, his speech, his piety, and his manner. His piety was without show or formality; his religious views were evangelical, yet his religious spirit was catholic and charitable. You will all bear testimony to his directness and unequivocacy of speech. Professor Walker always meant what he said, and he meant no more than he said; and when he had spoken we all felt that there was nothing ulterior, nothing dark or equivocal. His conscientiousness gave him oftentimes the appearance of severity. Duty with him was the first law; yet he required no more of another than he exacted of himself. Others might have found in feeble health like his an excuse from duty; yet he was seldom away from his post. He died in his armor; and in some sense may be said to be a martyr to his work.

It is fitting that we bring to the burial services of our beloved associate and instructor these floral tributes of affection—these wreaths and this crown. He is already crowned; crowned on earth with the labors of a useful life; and crowned in heaven with an everlasting crown, placed upon his brow by the hands of the adorable Redeemer. These flowers however which are so beautiful today shall fade and be thrown aside, but the memory of him whose funeral services they adorn shall be perennial.

How mysterious is his decease; the time of it—the University needs him; the manner of it—so unexpected, so sudden. Without the interpretation given by the divine oracles we can not solve the enigma of it; aye, aside from that interpretation all such bereavements as this are wholly inexplicable. What else shall give us their meaning? Today, we walk in paths that are plain and straight and free, the air is full of the song of birds, and the perfume of flowers; tomorrow we are struggling over roads that are rough and rugged and thorny, or forcing our way through the dark and fearful pass. Today there are bright skies above us, and vernal breezes fan our brow; tomorrow we are the prey of the pitiless storm. Now, we are in the midst of the most beloved society; soon, we are in dreary and dejected solitude. And we wonder sometimes whether God is a Father, or whether we are not all orphans and live in a fatherless world. But we are assured that this life is not the only life; that death is not the last of us; there is a land as pure as this is impure; as joyful as this is sad; as abiding as this is fugitive.

"There is a land of pure delight,
Where saints immortal reign."

It is said, that, on the shores of the Adriatic, the wives of th fishermen come down to the beach at eventide, and with their faces toward the sea on whose bosom their husbands are far away braving the perils of their calling, sing a stanza of a song well known to them both. When they have ended their song, waiting and listening, they hear borne on the wings of the wind, the next stanza of the song, sung by the distant husbands, responsive to their own. And both are happy and light-hearted. So might we hear, were our senses not so dull, from the far-off spirit land, songs responsive to our own—from forms unseen, but from voices known. "I ask them whence their victory came." "They with melted heart, ascribe their conquest to the Lamb, their triumph to his death."

Oh, there is a dreary, dangerous sea that separates us; but we may sing across it, and hear blessed voices in sympathy with our own and we are gladdened, and go to life's duties and burdens cheerfully—they may not come to us, but we may go to them.

Let us bear life's burdens, and perform its duties, as he did, whose decease we mourn today, thoughtfully and manfully, and go to our rest calmly and in the love of God.

REMARKS OF PROFESSOR CAMPBELL.

To express my appreciation of our departed friend I shall only say that among all my colleagues no one was respected by me more highly than Professor Walker. Indeed the uniqueness and nobility of his life seem to have found a culmination in these scenes which attend its close. The events of the past year have been wonderful. They have conspired to place a crown of glory upon his life-work.

Early in the autumn he had made his home in a fine, newly-finished residence—the product of his own industry. The occasion was complimented by a serenade from his classes, the students, in large number, taking this opportunity to manifest their respect and joy. But a few weeks ago he closed his superintendence of the schools in our division of the city. These schools had received, during his administration, a highly reputable character. With uncommon cordiality their teachers presented to him an enduring testimonial of their appreciation, which shall continue to speak in beautiful marble of his fidelity.

Just one week has passed since he closed his instruction of the junior class; and but a few hours before his departure, he was overjoyed to learn that, in his arduous labors as chairman of the Faculty Committee in a case of discipline in the University, which involved unusual difficulties, he had to the end the co-operation of his associates, and that the Faculty had been sustained by the Board of Regents.

After hearing this last communication, his mind seemed to be hovering between things temporal and the higher world. He fancies himself seated in assembly with his fellow-professors. He speaks softly. After a pause, he says audibly, "If there's no farther business, I move we adjourn." Who of us shall second the motion? When, if ever, shall we hold the next full meeting? We know not. One thing we do know, this faculty has *begun* to adjourn. When the last rollcall comes for each of us, may we be found ready to answer "Aye," and, thus answering, to sit down with our lamented brother, where the faithful rest and where no motion to "adjourn" shall ever be in order.

At another time during our friend's closing hours he seemed to be seated before his class. The recitation cheers him. He exclaims, "That's a beautiful translation." What "translation" did he mean? Did he catch a glimpse of the future—a "fore-gleam" of today, when he should himself personify *the* "translation"? A "beautiful translation," indeed!

A few years ago people supposed that the Latin was a dead language. The old Romans were in their tombs, and, of course, their speech was thought to be "dead" and gone. In these days, however, we appreciate the error. Human speech dieth not. It is lasting as the race. The Roman words have only changed their form—the toga for the gown—but they still speak.

So this, our friend, is not speechless. Though dead, he yet uttereth speech; and never before was he so eloquent as today.

Young men and young women, most of you have mastered his lessons in the past. Can you translate the lesson of this hour? Your much revered Professor now utters a universal language. Me thinks he seems to say: "*Tempora mutantur et nos in illis mutamur.*" "Times are changed and we are changed in them." Here indeed lies the earthly; it is the literal rendering,—"dust to dust." But there is a higher meaning, a "beautiful translation,"—"changed from glory into glory."

Let us heed the lesson of the day. I know well the purpose of my friend in teaching the young. He did not aim at showy results. With Professor Walker education meant the founding of character, the building up of noble men and women. You bear in your minds and hearts the workmanship of his discipline. The responsibility of his instructions is upon you. May you walk worthy of his example and of his words. In your lives may his wisdom and refinement be perpetuated. Then, surely his work shall not die. But, transmitted from tongue to tongue, from heart to heart, from character to character, from life to life, from generation to generation, there shall be fulfilled in you the words of his favorite poet, Virgil :

> "As long as the shadows move up and down the mountains,
> As long as the rivers wind their courses to the sea,
> As long as the stars gleam in the lofty sky,
> So long his name and his fame shall endure."

REMARKS OF PRESIDENT FOLWELL.

The University of Minnesota appears today for the first time as chief mourner at the burial of a loved and honored officer. But it is no idle ceremonial which brings her members to this house of prayer, and to the open tomb awaiting these remains. We join this sorrowing company of friends as fellow-mourners to mingle our tears with theirs. It has pleased God to take away our teacher, fellow-laborer and friend.

The University may well sorrow over her loss. The just man, the true friend, the skillful teacher was,—as he must have been—the trusted and useful professor, faithful, punctual, indefatigable, conscientious. Into the University he threw all the rich accumulations of many active and eventful years, learning—and wisdom which is better than learning,—culture, and a wide and varied experience.

His chosen department belonged to what scholars are wont to call "the humanities,"—and his teaching was indeed humanizing. Although devoted to his favorite subjects and authors he cared most for the minds and souls of his pupils. His chief thought never was, how much of this subject and lesson can I fix in these young minds, but how much can I help them through this subject to become men and women, noble and just and pure.

It was this personal, spiritual interest in character which won the abiding love and respect of all who sat under his instruction; and it is the remembrance of this which melts all our hearts today. It is this too, which gave permanence to his work; which will keep his influence fresh and potent for generations hence. This is the teachers' earthly reward.

I shall not attempt to estimate or weigh the loss the University has suffered. In one respect it cannot be repaired. No power can recover the seven years' experience which has closed. We can not fill that vacant chair in our councils by one, who from knowledge of the field and the work can advise so intelligently, so wisely, so kindly.

It has pleased God to afflict us. God's will be done. God give us strength and patience, and grace to heed the lesson of this day and hour; and when we shall have performed the last sad duty to our beloved friend let us return to our accustomed labors recalling the words of the great apostle: "Wherefore my beloved brethren, be ye steadfast, unmoveable, always abounding in the work of the Lord, inasmuch as ye know that your labor is not in vain in the Lord."

RESOLUTIONS OF THE BOARD OF REGENTS.

At a meeting of the Regents of the State University held on the 22d of June, 1876, the following resolutions were unanimously adopted, to-wit:

Resolved, That the sudden and unexpected demise of Professor V. J. Walker has caused a profound feeling of regret on the part of the members of this Board.

Resolved, That the long connection of the deceased with the University, his laborious and faithful services, his devotion to the best interests of this institution, his eminent scholarship, and his high character as a Christian teacher and gentleman, all combine to render his loss a calamity not only to the institution but to the entire State.

Resolved, That a copy of these resolutions be transmitted by the Secretary to the widow of the late Professor Walker, accompanied by a communication expressive of the deep sympathy felt by the Board in her bereavement, and that the resolutions be entered upon the minutes of this day's proceedings.

TESTIMONIALS FROM THE STATE TEACHERS' ASSOCIATION.

The Minnesota State Educational Association, held at Red Wing, August 22 and 23, 1876, ordered the following minutes to be entered in its records:

Although at the funeral of the late Prof. V. J. Walker, sketches of his character and work were given *in memoriam*, yet we, his fellow laborers, desire to place upon record a testimonial of our regards for him as a member of this association.

Mr. Walker was present at the first State Association of teachers held in Minnesota. He aided in the preparation of its constitution and contributed largely to the success of the meeting. Every year, with possibly one exception, he has attended our annual gatherings. While his characteristic modesty did not permit him to be a mover of many motions and a monopolizer of time in discussion, his few, but fitly spoken words always commanded attention. Having thought to good purpose, his quiet suggestions were of much value in directing business and reaching practical results.

It is with great satisfaction that we have witnessed his rise from a common school teacher to the merited position of Professor of the Latin language in our State University. May his unambitious success as a teacher incite us to fidelity in our work. May his death, sudden yet calm in faith and triumphant in hope, teach us all how to die.

D. BURT,
GEO C. SMITH,
H. B. WILSON,
Committee.

LETTER FROM HON. M. H. DUNNELL.

HOUSE OF REPRESENTATIVES,
Washington, D. C., May 21, 1876.

MRS. V. J. WALKER: Dear Madam,—I cannot lessen your grief at the death of your dear husband; but permit me to assure you of my sincere sympathy and my own great sadness at his too early departure.

You are aware of our college relations, and of our undisturbed friendship. It was my privilege to recommend Mr. Walker for the place in the University which he filled with so much honor. As his classmate, I knew of his exact scholarship; and as a school officer, I had witnessed his eminent qualities as an instructor. I did not err in my recommendation; my interest in the University was heightened by his connection with it. My interest and respect for him increased as he increased in years. I feel very deeply his loss. You alone can measure yours. God can be praised in the midst of afflictions, for we know that He always does well.

If present, Mrs. Dunnell and my family would unite in these words of sympathy.

Yours very truly,

M. H. DUNNELL.

TESTIMONIALS FROM THE BOARD OF EDUCATION IN WINONA.

The death of Versal J. Walker, formerly teacher, principal, and Superintendent of Schools in the city of Winona, and later an honored professor of the Latin language in the State University at Minneapolis, having been announced in regular session and motion made for such action by the Board as should be deemed proper, the Board thereupon

Resolved, That this Board have heard with profound sorrow of the death of Professor Walker, and desire to record this their testimonial to his worth, and their regard for his memory:

He was one whose search was for sound, practical knowledge; who was always ready to assist others in the search; who to that end became a successful organizer and teacher of common schools; who carried a ripe experience to the aid of the State University; and whose valuable counsels were freely given to every public educational work.

He believed that well directed hard work is the only sure means of valuable acquirements; that correct habits both of body and mind are essential to effective work; and that a wise but firm discipline, as promotive of correct habits, is equally necessary with correct methods in order to human development.

This Board recognize that to his patient labor, constant watchfulness, and practical application of these principles during almost a decade, the schools of the city of Winona owe a large share of their success and usefulness, and that this work is a prouder and more enduring tribute to his memory than marble monuments.

Being without ostentation, his works only remain to testify of him, but they tell of the faithful and wise teacher, the warm friend and loving husband, the good citizen and the honest man.

To this record this Board in deep sympathy venture to point the bereft wife as a source of comfort; while to his former pupils and his co-workers such a record is worthy of the most profound emulation

Resolved, That these proceedings be spread upon the records of this Board and that a copy be furnished to the widow of the deceased, and to the press for publication.

By the Board of Education of the City of Winona.

J. M. COLE, Clerk.

RESOLUTION OF THE MINNESOTA BAPTIST ASSOCIATION.

The following resolution was passed at a recent meeting of the Minnesota Baptist Association held at Hastings:

Resolved, That we have heard with profound regret and sorrow of the death of Professor V. J. Walker, of the State University; and that we desire to express our high appreciation of Professor Walker's character as a Christian man, and of his great usefulness as an educator; and that we hereby express to Mrs. Walker our heartfelt sympathy in this her great sorrow.

E. W. VANDUZEE,
Moderator.

LYMAN PALMER,
Clerk.

HYMN SUNG AT THE GRAVE.

HE SWEETLY SLEEPS.

I

Sleep thy last sleep, free from care and sorrow;
Rest where none weep, till th' eternal morrow:
Tho' dark waves roll, o'er the silent river,
Thy fainting soul, Jesus can deliver.

II

Life's dream is past, all its sin and sadness;
Brightly at last, dawns the day of gladness;
Under thy sod, earth, receive our treasure,—
To rest in God, waiting all his pleasure.

III

Tho' we may mourn those in life the dearest,
They shall return, Christ, when thou appearest!
Soon shall thy voice comfort those now weeping,
Bidding rejoice all in Jesus sleeping.

—*Perkins' Anthem Book.*

Citizen Steam Press, Academy of Music.

www.ingramcontent.com/pod-product-compliance
Lightning Source LLC
LaVergne TN
LVHW011144110826
845150LV00008B/2497
* 9 7 8 1 4 1 8 1 9 2 3 9 6 *